Acknowledgements

D0824064

We would like to thank all of the students who contributed their ideas and experiences, and whose unflagging enthusiasm for this project helped to validate the need for this book. Peggy Prinz, from Study Abroad USA, was most encouraging in her support and endorsement. We would also like to thank our professional colleagues, whose interest in addressing international students' concerns inspired many lively discussions and exchange of ideas.

Thanks too to Peter Stevens, President of Cambridge Stratford Study Skills Institute for his advice, interest, and support throughout the process of gathering information, writing, and producing our work.

Finally, our husbands, Leonard Rothman and Michael Kolko, spent many hours assisting us with preparing survey forms, collating research, and reading and rereading our manuscript.

Who Are The Authors?

Dr. Juliet Rothman teaches in the School of Social Welfare and in the School of Public Health at the University of California at Berkeley. One of her areas of specialization is diversity, and she has interviewed and advised students from abroad, new immigrants, and students from minority populations for many years. She has traveled extensively world-wide and is fluent in several languages. Dr. Rothman holds Master's degrees in both Social Work and Liberal Education, and a doctorate in Philosophy from American University. She has also taught at Catholic University and American University in Washington DC.

Ms. Kolko teaches at American InterContinental University in Los Angeles. American InterContinental University has schools throughout the world and specializes in working with international students. One of her areas of specialization is University Success and she has taught and advised students from abroad for many years. Ms. Kolko holds a Bachelor of Science degree from Syracuse University and a Master's degree in Organizational Development from Antioch University. She has traveled extensively outside of the United States.

Introduction

Attention! Please read this before going forward.

Attending college in the USA offers unparalleled opportunities to international students. Many of these are well known to you and, no doubt, influenced your decision to pursue your education in the US.

100 Things Every International Student Ought to Know was written to help you experience those opportunities with more satisfaction and success. Just like a foreign traveler to a new location for business or vacation, an international student needs to know how to navigate, not only in getting from place to place, but also in making effective decisions on a day-to-day basis. Critical to such decisions is having the right information.

In writing **100 Things**, informal surveys with hundreds of international students provided a focus on many of the more meaningful topics that proved an aid in college adjustment, persistence, and success through graduation. Many of the suggestions heard were helpful and relevant, yet had not been published in a single source orientation and problem-solving guidebook for international students.

100 Things is designed to get you thinking as early as possible about the WHAT, WHY, WHERE, WHEN, and HOW of completing your own self-orientation to college. To further assist you, an appendix was added to include actual comments of international students in the US, a glossary of terms and phrases used in the US, references and readings you may find helpful for further discovery. A wealth of helpful websites that further expand your opportunities for learning has also been included..

Our goal is to provide a better understanding of what studying in the US is really about. Just as in other countries, rules and regulations are critical to learn, understand, and follow. However, studying in the US also provides freedoms, rights, and opportunities that can make your experience widely different. The key to a quick adjustment is 1) aware-

ness and 2) self-discovery. **100 Things** attempts to accomplish the first and its authors' hope it encourages you to accomplish the second.
We wish you well in your adjustment and ultimate success. We are grateful for this opportunity to help you in this new transition in your life. Good luck in stepping forward in this new challenge before you. We hope ***100 Things Every International Student Ought to Know*** helps you on your journey.

Juliet C. Rothman
Susan R. Kolko

Table of Contents

1 Legal Rights and Responsibilites in School and Work

International Students Ought to Know:

1.   It is **your personal responsibility to keep your visa and documents valid at all times.** US law requires that all international students have a lawful immigration status. The Certificate of Eligibility sent by your school when you were accepted includes an 11-digit number which is your official admission number, registered with the INS. It's important to keep track of that number and to use it for all visa-related matters.

International Students Ought to Know:

2.   that **there are two main visa categories** for international students and scholars. Full-time students use the F-1 visa category. Researchers and visiting scholars use the J-1 category. The category to which you are assigned depends on what you will be doing at your school, and there are slight variations between the two groupings.

International Students Ought to Know:

3.   that **your "immigration documents" include**:

F-1 Visas:
   a. Passport
   b. Certificate of Eligibility (Form F-20), which includes an "end date"—a date by which it is presumed you will have completed your studies in the United States.
   c. Departure Record (INS form I-94, stapled into your passport)

*Your F-1 visa stamp does not need to be valid at all times while you are in the United States; however, it must be valid if you leave the United States and wish to re-enter.

J-1 Visas:
   a. Passport
   b. Certificate of Eligibility (USIA form IAP-66), which includes an "end date".
   c. Departure Record (INS form I-94, stapled into your passport)

International Students Ought to Know:

4.   that since the **terrorist attacks of September 11, 2001, the visa application process has become more difficult and time consuming,** and you may experience a delay in both the application process and in making changes or special arrangements. Plan extra time for this!!

International Students Ought to Know:

5.   that **your school's international student office (ISSO) is the quickest and best source of information about your visa**, and should be the first place you contact with questions. However, *this is not an official INS office.* If you have a special problem or question, you must ask an INS official in the federal INS office.

You also have the right to consult an attorney specializing in immigration law if you have any special concerns. The cost of this consultation is your personal responsibility.

International Students Ought to Know:

6.   that **you must contact the ISSO office at your school at least a month ahead of time to let them know if you plan to return home** for a visit or vacation to request travel authorization. An official from the office will stamp your I-20 or IAP-66 form, and you will be given a special Travel Form. The stamp is valid for a year, except for travel to Canada, Mexico, or adjoining islands, where it is valid for six months only. When you return, visit the ISSO again and let them know you are back, so they can update your files.

You can return home to visit at any time. You can also travel freely within the United States, with your **valid** passport, Certificate of Eligibility, and Departure record.

Make copies of all of your documents and keep them in a safe place. If the originals are lost or stolen, copies will facilitate their replacement.

International Students Ought to Know:

7.   that **since the terrorist attacks, overview of foreign nationals living in the US has become more intense**, and is the responsibility of both the INS and the new Department of Homeland Security. You will experience delays in processing visa-related materials; you may be individually monitored more closely; you may experience difficulty in renewing or extending your visa; and, if you are from certain countries or areas of the world, you may be interviewed or questioned regarding potential terrorist activities.

While this may be upsetting and offensive, it is important to remember that you are not *personally* being investigated or supervised. These are general policies designed to ensure the overall safety and security of everyone in the United States, whether citizen, resident, or temporary visitor.

International Students Ought to Know:

8.   your student **visa is valid until the completion of your studies or the expiration of your visa, whichever occurs first**. Your completion date is the day of your graduation, and you can stay in the US for up to thirty days after that date. You can extend this up to sixty days if your visa stamp remains current, but no longer. To stay in the US longer, you must either begin a new program of studies; apply for "academic training" employment (OPT—see next item); or change your immigration status.

International Students Ought to Know:

9.   you can **stay in the US for 12 months after you complete your studies if you get employment related to your academic study and goals and have an F-1 visa**. You can request optional practical training (OPT) with the INS through your school's ISSO after you complete full-time study. To apply for this program, your graduation date must be on your university records (you must be "cleared" for graduation and have met all of the school's requirements), or you must have a letter from your adviser attesting to your expected date of graduation. You can apply for OPT anytime between 120 days prior to graduation to 60 days after graduation, but schools prefer early application.

International Students Ought to Know:

10. your visa is registered and tracked when you enter the US on an F-1 or J-1 visa using SEVIS, the Student and Exchange Visitor Information Service. As of January, 2003, all educational institutions must report and keep current the status of all international students attending their institutions. International students are required to pay a fee, currently $95. directly to the Attorney General's office for their registration in the SEVIS system before student classifications are assigned.

All the information required by SEVIS has been law in the United States for a long time, and is not a new, post 9/11 requirement. The SEVIS system centralizes and coordinates information, so that it is more accessible to government agencies. After your school has registered you with SEVIS, you will be issued an I-20 Form which is SEVIS-compatible.

International Students Ought to Know:

11. **SEVIS will register**:

   a. Your name, place and date of birth, country of citizenship, current address, and student visa classification.

   b. Your port of entry and date of entry

   c. Your academic status (full or part-time), any academic disciplinary actions taken against you, the date of commencement of your studies, your degree program and field of study, practical training, with beginning and ending dates, number of credits completed per year

   d. Your termination date from any program and the reasons for your termination

   e. Your I-20 information

International Students Ought to Know:

12. that your **school will use the Internet to provide and update information with SEVIS**. All the information will be maintained in a central data base by the BCIS. (Bureau of Citizenship and Immigration Service). Some schools can maintain a local database with information about the international students enrolled in their programs.

International Students Ought to Know:

13. that you need to **keep your visa current**, report any changes in your status, and get the proper forms for travel, employment, visa extensions, etc. to keep current with the INS (Immigration and Naturalization Service) and BCIS (Bureau of Citizenship and Immigration Service). Your ISSO office knows all the procedures and can help you. You can also go directly to an INS office if you have questions or concerns.

International Students Ought to Know:

14. that if you need to take time off from your studies, **an official leave of absence from your school won't protect your student visa status**. You will lose your student visa if you do not register for a semester (excluding summer, unless your program begins with or includes summer studies), withdraw from your program during the semester, or if you are suspended from your program.

The only allowable exception to this is an interruption of studies due to a medical condition which renders study impossible. If you have special family circumstances that necessitate interrupting your studies, contact your ISSO as soon as you become aware of the problem. They may be able to help you to get an exception for this reason.

Your financial aid will also terminate when you interrupt your studies. You have to re-apply both for financial aid and a student visa in order to resume your studies. Be sure to allow plenty of time for these applications!

International Students Ought to Know:

15. that if **you want to transfer, and are accepted at another school, your new school will send you a Certificate of Eligibility** for that school. Contact the ISSO offices of both your old and new school to help you with the transfer process. If there is a break in your full-time study during the transfer process, your visa eligibility will be affected.

Each school and program has its own requirements for course work, grades, and content. You can apply to transfer credits from one institution to another, but shouldn't expect that all your credits will transfer. Generally, there is a minimum number of credits which must be taken at the degree-granting institution. Grades which are below a certain level will not transfer.

International Students Ought to Know:

16. that you must **have good academic standing in order to keep your student visa**. You should not be on probation or be expelled, and should have a passing grade point average (GPA). What constitutes "passing" varies from school to school, but if your GPA falls below your school's level, you will be put on probation for one or more semesters. During this probationary period, you will be expected to demonstrate that you are able to do the work required by your program with good grades.

If you continue to receive failing grades, you will be expelled from school.

If you are at risk of probation or of being expelled, it is important that you contact your academic adviser to get help. Special workshops, programs, tutoring, and other resources can help you get back "on track."

International Students Ought to Know:

17. that you **have to let the ISSO know of any changes in your program or your major**, and both your F-20 form and the SEVIS system must be updated to reflect the change.

Changing your program or your major may also affect the expected date of completion of your studies.

International Students Ought to Know:

18. that if you **are in the US on an F-1 visa, you are required to engage in "full-time study"**. While each school or program can define this differently, "full-time" generally means at least 12 semester hours for graduate and undergraduate students. "Audits" (classes you attend but for which you do not receive a grade) don't count toward this requirement.

The number of credits each course carries varies by the number of hours it meets each week. If your school is on the semester system, two credit courses generally meet for two hours, three credit courses for three hours, and so forth. Science courses often carry four or five credits, especially when labs are required in addition to classes. In effect, if you are taking science courses you will be taking fewer courses, but the demands and credits of each course will be greater.

International Students Ought to Know:

19. that **if you are a doctoral student, have completed all of your course work, and are working on your dissertation, you can register for less than the required 12 credits and still maintain full-time status**. You will need a letter attesting to this from your department each semester. If you can't complete your dissertation in the time originally planned, you can apply for a visa extension through your ISSO. The change in expected completion date will be registered on your I-20 form, and also with SEVIS.

International Students Ought to Know:

20. that if you **enrolled in a program that begins with a summer semester or includes a summer semester requirement, you must register for summer in order to keep your student visa current**. If you began your program of studies in the fall semester, summer study is not required.

During the summer, you can travel both within the US or abroad, or apply for employment through Curricular Practical Training (CPT) internship programs at your school.

International Students Ought to Know:

21. that the **US government requires you to demonstrate financial assets to cover the expenses** of your program as well as living expenses before you begin your studies. Work opportunities are often limited for international students, and evidence that you can pay for your schooling and living expenses assures the government that you will not become dependent upon government resources and be able to complete your program.

International Students Ought to Know:

22.   that if **you have financial problems while you are here, you may apply for loans, or be employed under specific regulations and terms as a student**. It's best to avoid problems and plan carefully before you begin; but, if an emergency need occurs, go to your ISSO for advice and assistance. There are some exceptions to the employment restrictions which can assist you to earn a portion of your expenses.

You should also check on additional grants and funding for which you may be eligible through your own country. Many countries will provide assistance to their citizens who are studying abroad but plan to return and use their knowledge in their country.

International Students Ought to Know:

23. that your **student visa restricts you to on-campus employ-ment of 20 hours or less a week**. There are three ways to obtain exceptions to this:

  1. You can apply for special authorization to work off campus because of financial hardship or because there are no jobs available on campus. You will need to fill out Form OMB 1115-0163 and OMB 115-0060 to apply for this exemption through the International Students' Office.
  2. You can apply for Curricular Practical Training (see next item).
  3. You can apply for special permission if you are from certain Pacific rim countries (see #24).

International Students Ought to Know:

24. that **Curricular Practical Training (CPT) is an internship or practicum program which is related to your field of studies** and offered through your school. You can do CPT over school vacations, in the summer, while school is in session, while you are writing your thesis or dissertation, or after you have completed your formal studies. It is limited to one year of full-time employment, and weeks are cumulative over the entire course of your program. To be eligible, you must have completed at least nine months of a degree program. You'll need a "Curricular Practical Training Recommendation" from your adviser. Schedule an appointment with an ISSO adviser and bring: the recommendation form, your passport, your I-20 form, INS Form I-538. Your ISSO adviser must approve your employment and authorize this on your I-20 form.

International Students Ought to Know:

25. that if you **are from Korea, Malaysia, Thailand, Indonesia, or the Philippines you can apply for permission to work more than 20 hours a week**, and can also apply for a reduced course load in order to work these additional hours. You can't decrease your course load until your application has been authorized. The permission is valid for one year or until you complete your program or studies. You'll also need to fill out a personal statement, and complete forms OMB 111501 and OMB 11150060.

International Students Ought to Know:

26. that if **you are employed in the United States, you need a valid Social Security card**. Apply for a card at the Social Security Administration Office. Your application must include an I-20 form (for F-1 students) or by IAP 66 and an Employment Authorization Document (for J-2 students). While cards are generally issued within 14 days of application, you may experience a delay due to more rigorous processes initiated after the terrorist attacks.

To get information about social security cards in your native language, go to www.ssa.gov/multilanguage/indexhtm.

International Students Ought to Know:

27. that **all residents in the US**—permanent or temporary, citizen or non-citizen, employed or not employed—**must file both Federal and State tax returns** on an annual basis, as well as city and county tax returns in some areas. All students in F-1 and J-1 visa categories are included in this requirement.

Tax forms may be downloaded from the federal Internal Revenue site and from state and local government sites, and are also available in Post Offices and public government offices. Your ISSO office may also have forms available for your convenience. Most tax returns are due by April 15th each year.

International Students Ought to Know:

28. that **if you are married, you may be able to have your spouse and children accompany you while you are studying** in the US. Your family's visa category will reflect your own: if you have an F-1 visa, your spouse and dependents may apply for an F-2 visa; if you have a J-1 visa, they may apply for a J-2 visa.

It's easier for you to get their visas if they are filed with the US embassy in your country at the same time as your own. Bring their birth and marriage certificates with you when you apply. If you are applying for their visas at a later date, include documentation of your student visa status with your family members' applications.

International Students Ought to Know:

29. that your **spouse can work in the US as long as the income is *not* used for your education or support**, but is only supplementary income. You must support yourself with personal funds, scholarships and grants, and your own employment, but not through the employment of a spouse or dependents. The income dependents earn can be used for educational, recreational, and cultural activities only.

Take a cover letter asking for employment authorization and noting that the income from such employment will not be used to support you, visa status documentation, two photographs to be used for an employment card, a check for the $120 fee, and your dependent with you to your ISSO office. After your material has been reviewed by the ISSO, you will be directed to send the material to your regional INS Service Center.

It should take 6-8 weeks to receive the employment authorization.

A Social Security card is necessary for all employment in the US. Apply through the Social Security Administration for cards for family members.

International Students Ought to Know:

30. that **if your country and the US have strained relations, there can be a longer delay in the processing** of your visa application and of any changes and updates. Your records will be checked more thoroughly, your activities will be monitored more closely, and you may be requested to come for interviews or to provide additional information. Since the terrorist attacks in New York and Washington, federal officers have been given new powers to arrest, detain, and question. The ACLU suggests that you carry with you the name and telephone number of a lawyer who specializes in working with foreign nationals in the United States. You have the right to call your lawyer if you are detained.

International Students Ought to Know:

31.   that a big **legal issue in the US that may affect you is "profiling"**—using race, religion, country of origin, or other criteria to determine if a person or a group of people should be treated differently than others based on suspicions of possible terrorist or criminal activity. Until and unless this issue is resolved, you may encounter differential treatment if you are from certain areas of the world.

People in the United States have become more suspicious and less trusting since the terrorist attacks on September 11th, 2001. It is important to recognize that people's reactions are not addressed toward you as an individual, and that the motivation is fear, rather than dislike.

International Students Ought to Know:

32.   that **if your visa is revoked, you may be asked to leave** the country. If you agree to leave voluntarily, you may be waiving your right to appeal and to go before a judge. If you want to appeal, ask a lawyer who specializes in visa issues to review your individual circumstances and offer professional advice. The lawyer will charge a fee for this service.

International Students Ought to Know:

33. that **there are lawyers who specialize in immigration law** and who can help you with problems with visas, and other legal issues. You can find a lawyer through their professional organization, Immigration Lawyers Association, online at AILA.org

International Students Ought to Know:

34. your **brothers and sisters can apply for a Tourist Visa to visit the US** through the embassy in your country if they want to come and visit you. The ISSO office at your school can assist in this process by giving you a Letter of Invitation to include with their application.

2 Knowing College/Course Requirements and Student Services

International Students Ought to Know:

35.   that **your school has a special department which addresses special concerns of international students**. We've used ISSO (International Students and Scholars) as the general name for this department in our book, but yours may be called the International Students' Office, Department of International Programs/Students, or various other titles. The "International" is the key word to look for in a campus directory if you are trying to locate the service.

Generally, the ISSO will reach out to you—they know you are there!

International Students Ought to Know:

36.   Most **ISSO's can help you with**:

Visas	ESL courses
Employment	Activities, clubs and organizations
Health and Medical Issues	Community contacts
Marriage and Partnering	Living Arrangements
Legal Matters	Traveling within and out of the country

They can only help you if you go there—this should be one of your very first campus stops!!

International Students Ought to Know:

37.   about **good people to talk to about academic stuff**: other students in your program, especially upperclasspersons; graduate students in your field; tutors; mentors, if your school has a mentoring program; your adviser; a counselor from the school's Counseling Office; someone from the ISSO, a staff member in the department in which you are studying. Don't forget your family—they are a good resource too!

International Students Ought to Know:

38. that you should **plan your schedule** so that all your school's required courses are included. Because everybody must take these, they fill quickly. Plan to take them well before your expected graduation date. If you think you may be transferring to another educational institution, take basic requirements first: not all credits transfer and basic courses transfer more easily than more specialized courses.

University-wide course requirements generally apply only to undergraduate students, and may include: a foreign language requirement, a science requirement, a physical education requirement, a diversity or multi-cultural content requirement, an English requirement, and a CPR (cardio-pulmonary resusitation) requirement. Each of these courses carry credits which are a part of the total number of credits required for graduation.

International Students Ought to Know:

39.   that **you'll have a period of time, as long as two years at some schools, to decide on your major**. When you "declare" a major, you'll be assigned a faculty adviser in your field to help you plan your program. Each department has requirements for majors, such as: a minimum number of courses in that field; a certain grade-point average in major courses, a number of courses at an advanced level which have "prerequisites" (courses which must be taken ahead of the advanced course), courses in related subjects; and specific courses in the department. You also must take a certain number of credits, determined by your school, in your major field.

Some schools also require, or allow, students to declare a "minor." Minors can be in a related field, such as biology and chemistry, or in a separate field, such as French and music. Minors also have course and credit requirements, but these are generally much fewer than major requirements. Some schools permit students to carry two majors, called "double majors." If you "declare" majors in two fields, you will be expected to meet the full major requirements for each one.

International Students Ought to Know:

40. that **if you change your major, you'll have to meet all major requirements in your new field**. If you've changed to something similar to your original choice, you may be able to transfer some credits to meet the new major's requirements. If you are changing to something completely different, you will need to start all over again to accumulate the required number of major credits in your new major. The later you decide to change majors, the more potential there is that it will affect your graduation date. Changing majors during your last year will almost certainly delay graduation by a semester, a year, or

more, and you will be scrambling to take required courses at the last minute.

If changes in your program delay your expected date of completion of studies, you must immediately contact the ISSO office on your campus and the INS, and follow the procedures for requesting a student visa extension. Remember too, that you will need to carry a full-time course load to maintain your student visa status. Also, your change in major must also be registered with SEVIS through your school's ISSO.

International Students Ought to Know:

41. that a **GPA, or grade point average, is your average grade based on the number of credits you have taken**. Because courses carry different numbers of credits, the effect of any one grade on your GPA will vary.   An A in a three credit course will affect your GPA more than an A in a two-credit course, less than an A in a four-credit course.

Based on overall GPA, and/or on number of credits below a certain level, your university's policies will determine: whether you are qualified to graduate, whether you will be placed on probation, whether you will be expelled for academic reasons, or whether you will graduate with honors.

International Students Ought to Know:

42. that letter **grades range from A to F** and may or may not include pluses and minuses, depending on your school. A to F grades are based on a four point system. Most schools use a conversion table like this:

A = 4.0	B+ = 3.3	C+ = 2.3	D+ = 1.3	F = 0
A- = 3.7	B = 3.0	C = 2.0	D = 1.0	
	B- = 2.7	C- = 1.7	D- = .7	

It is important for you to remember that there are grade-point minimums which must be met in order to maintain your student visa, and also to qualify for scholarships and financial aid!

International Students Ought to Know:

43. that **good English writing and speaking skills will help you** to get a better grade. To work on these, contact your school's ISSO, counseling office, or learning center to learn about ESL courses and study and writing skills workshops. You may also engage a private tutor to assist you.

International Students Ought to Know:

44. that **you are expected to attend class, to arrive on time and with your learning materials, to have done the required readings and assignments, to listen attentively and respectfully, and to participate in classroom discussions and exercises**. You should not talk to other students, have your cell phone on, fall asleep, or eat or drink without the consent of the instructor. You are expected to remain in the classroom and not enter and leave at will.

High achievers tend to sit toward the front of the classroom.

International Students Ought to Know:

45. that **many instructors take attendance** during every class. Be sure you know each instructor's policies about attendance and participation: they may be part of your course grade. Let your professor know ahead of time if you will be unable to attend a class, be sure to do your reading, and get notes about what was taught from a fellow student.

Instructors lecture on material not covered in the readings, and you will be tested on this material. Class discussions stimulate new ideas and learning, and classroom exercises can help you understand difficult material.

International Students Ought to Know:

46. that in some schools, **attendance records are kept as a part of your permanent record** and are used to evaluate your overall performance, motivation, level of effort, and interest in your work. Poor attendance records may affect your applications for internships, employment, and advanced study.

International Students Ought to Know:

47. that **you are expected to participate in classes** unless they are large lectures. Students learn from each other as well as from the professor, and the reasonable opinions and ideas of each student are valued and respected.

You may feel uncomfortable with this because you may feel self-conscious about your English, or unsure that you have understood the material well. You may be shy, or come from a culture where students are expected to listen and not speak. You may be uncomfortable expressing your ideas in public. If the expectation is that each student will participate, you should talk with your professor and explain your concerns and your discomfort.

International Students Ought to Know:

48. that **the course outline you get the first day of class is your guide for the course**, and you should use it as a reference each week. Course outlines usually include:

a.   a general description of the course,

b.   what you are expected to know and be able to do when you've completed the course,

c.   the course format: lecture, discussion, use of videos, speakers, etc.,

d. the grading system that will be used,
e. a description of each assignment: guidelines, due dates, paper length, type of exams,
f. a list of required and recommended textbooks,
g. a class-by-class guide which includes: the subject of the class, the reading assignments, and any other expected preparation (do your reading **before** the date on the outlines), and
h. policies about attendance and lateness.

International Students Ought to Know:

49. that **some instructors ask you to sign a "learning contract"** when you begin a course. There are several things that may be a part of the contract: your statement of your own learning goals, the goals for the course as a whole, special assignments and expectations, etc. You may also be asked to sign a statement that you understand the assignments and requirements of the course. Be sure that you do, before you sign!

International Students Ought to Know:

50. that **individual contacts with professors are encouraged in the US**. All professors have "office hours"—times during the week when they are available to students, with or without appointments, to discuss the course or any problem you may be having with school. Early in the semester, stop by your professor's office and introduce yourself. Explain that you are an international student, and share any concerns you have about class, papers, exams, or other issues. A personal contact helps

your professor to know you and to address your individual learning needs and concerns.

You can return to office hours as needed, and can call the professor's office during office hours if you are unable to get there in person. You can also use e-mail, especially if you have questions about an assignment or a reading. Most professors respond to e-mails in a timely manner.

International Students Ought to Know:

51. that if your professor does not have regular office hours, **you can request a meeting on an individual basis**, or talk with him or her briefly before or after class and during breaks. If your professor gives a home phone number to the class, it is OK to call—just be sure you call between 9 AM and 9 PM.

Your professor will let the class know how she or he prefers to be addressed. There is a great variation in styles—some prefer the formal "Professor" or "Doctor" title, while others prefer that students call them by their first names.

International Students Ought to Know:

52. that **if you're having trouble understanding because your professor speaks too quickly for you, office hours are a good time and place to let him or her know** about your problem. Changing your seat might help too. Double-check your notes with a classmate to be sure you've understood if you're not sure about something. You can also request permission to tape record lectures and listen to them again after class.

International Students Ought to Know:

53. that **students are expected to be able to demonstrate mastery of material** by their ability to recall and use the information they have learned without the assistance of textbooks, study guides, or other aides. Grades are based on knowledge and not on the ability to use resources, although this is also an important asset. Exams are generally written, and require a mixture of recall and application, analysis and synthesis. A multiple-choice computer card, short answers, fill in the blanks,

essays, or any combination of these methods can be used by your professor during exams.

While you can't take texts or notes into exams with you, it is important to study these thoroughly in advance. Special study guides, study groups, and note-taking services with instructor approval can help you to prepare for exams.

International Students Ought to Know:

54. that **sometimes teachers use other kinds of exams**. These include:

a. oral exams: rarely used except for doctoral students,

b. "open-book" exams: where you are allowed to take textbooks and other course material with you to the examination,

c. "take-home" exams: where the exam is given to you in advance and you have time to respond to the questions and exercises at home, turning your answers in to the instructor during the next class meeting, and

d. "paper options": where you have a choice of taking an examination or writing a paper on a pre-selected topic.

International Students Ought to Know:

55. "Cheating" includes using any method other than your own knowledge and skill to obtain information asked on an examination, and carries penalties which may include being expelled from school. Looking at a neighbor's paper, passing notes, looking at notes strategically placed within view, writing notes on your hand or clothing, asking another student for an answer, using electronic databases, and plagiarism are all types of cheating. Helping someone else is considered cheating also.

Examinations are "proctored" to prevent cheating. Your professor and assistants will monitor you while you take exams. You may be asked to sit in alternate seats, or in a special arrangement to help prevent cheating.

International Students Ought to Know:

56. that **students who are caught cheating receive a failing grade for the course, and may not continue to attend class**. Cheating is reported to your adviser and to the school administration. You may be expelled, placed on probation, or otherwise penalized for cheating. Your overall scholastic record will be affected.

Cheating is a very serious infraction. You may be expelled, lose your student visa, compromise your entire education, and lose references, employment, and other privileges if you are caught cheating or assisting someone else to cheat on examinations.

International Students Ought to Know:

57.   that **you can lose points on your exam if you do not use correct grammar and spelling**. To avoid this problem, take courses and attend workshops which teach English writing skills.

If you are currently having problems with English, and are trying to address these, let your professor know **before** you take an exam. Some professors won't deduct points if they know you are working on your writing skills and are aware that this is important.

International Students Ought to Know:

58. that **if you think you weren't graded fairly on an exam, the first step to take is to discuss your problem with the professor**. Present clear reasons for thinking you were not graded fairly, and be specific about questions, responses, and details. The professor may agree to change the grade, or you may agree that the professor's reasoning is valid.

If you still believe your grade is unfair, ask for an appointment with the department chairperson or dean. Each department has system for addressing this problem. Usually, a committee will review your exam and the grade assigned, and make recommendations to the professor. The professor has the final decision-making power, however, and may refuse to change a grade.

International Students Ought to Know:

59. that **students who go to office hours before exams often are given a good orientation to the exam** and what might be included!

International Students Ought to Know:

60. that **to get the best possible grade on an exam, you should**:

a. Make outlines of material on 5 by 7 index cards. Review these every week, and divide them into "I know" and "I need to learn" piles.

b. Join a study group of students in your class.

c. Make a master outline. The *process* of making the outline will help you learn.

d. Study every week, so that at exam time you'll only be reviewing and not learning material for the first time.

e. Start preparing early. Last-minute studying leaves you exhausted for the exam.

f. Ask your professor to review anything you don't understand in class or at office hours.

g. Get a good nights' sleep, and eat nutritious meals so that your mind and body are functioning at their best.

International Students Ought to Know:

61. that **the term "research" can mean looking up material in the library, using electronic databases and the Internet, interviewing people, doing surveys, doing experiments, developing systems and testing them, and many other activities**. Each field of study has a variety of different research methods and tools that are specific to that field.

A **research paper** asks you to use outside material, gather sources and references, analyze them, and present them in an organized and cohesive way. Generally, you begin with an idea—something which can be proved or disproved, explored, and deliberated upon, and use research to examine the validity of that idea, or as the foundation for developing a new idea or concept.

International Students Ought to Know:

62. that when you are doing research, **it is essential to develop a system for keeping track of the information you are gathering**. You can use index cards, paper, computerized systems, etc. **Don't** rely on your memory: there's too much information. Record all of your findings as you go along, including sources and bibliographical information, page numbers, and chart references. Keep all of the survey tools, actual surveys, experiment records, and any other data organized and in a safe place, so that you will be able to access them easily when you begin to analyze what you have learned. Develop an outline that describes your research process, reasoning, and conclusions before you begin to write.

International Students Ought to Know:

63. that **professors generally have very clear ideas about how they want papers to be organized**. Generally, you will be given guidelines; if you are not, ask for instructions in class or by meeting with your instructor privately.

Follow your professor's guidelines carefully: you'll be graded on each of the expected content areas, and, if you omit one, you won't get credit for that section. Following the outline and using sections and subtitles will make it easier for your professor to grade your paper, and help you to get a good grade.

International Students Ought to Know:

64. that **outlines for papers generally should include**:
a. an introductory statement,
b. the body of the paper, divided into sections and subsections clearly marked with titles, numbers, or other systems,
c. charts, graphs, or other supporting materials,
d. a summary, and
e. a bibliography.

Prepare your outline before you begin to write your paper. If you are unsure about your paper's structure and content, ask your professor to review it before you begin writing.

Keep your bibliography current as you write to avoid leaving out important sources!

International Students Ought to Know:

65. that **it is essential to give credit to other authors when you use them in your writing**. Professors know the writing style of each student, and can tell if you are using material written by someone else.

The next few items will show you how to do this.

International Students Ought to Know:

66. that **there are two places in your paper where you recognize the work of others: the bibliography, and the footnote**. The bibliography   appears at the end of the paper. Footnotes, which are also called "attributions," appear in the body of your paper, in all of the places where outside material is used.

"Attribution" separates your work from someone else's and recognizes the work of the other person. Attribution is essential in all scholarly work in the US. If you fail to correctly attribute material you have used from other sources, you may be accused of cheating or plagiarism and be expelled from school, so you must be very careful when you use such material.

International Students Ought to Know:

67. that **plagiarism is regarded as a very severe infraction**. This includes using material from other sources and having papers written by others. Any material presented as your own which is not original with you is plagiarism.

Professors often use professional services to check student work for plagiarism. If you are caught, you will be expelled from school, and lose your student visa. There are no "second chances" or excuses accepted.

International Students Ought to Know:

68. When you are writing a paper, **outside material which is paraphrased or summarized is included in the body of your paper**. The sentence in which the material is presented is followed by the attribution in parentheses. For example, if you were writing about attributions and you got the material from here, you might say:

It is important to include attributions when using outside sources (Rothman & Kolko, 2004).

International Students Ought to Know:

69. When you are writing a paper, **outside material which is directly reproduced must be placed within quotation marks, and be followed by an attribution**. For example, you may write:

"Attribution is essential to all scholarly work in the United States" (Rothman & Kolko, 2004).

International Students Ought to Know:

70. When you are writing a paper, and use **directly reproduced material which is longer**—a paragraph, for example—you can form the body of the paper by narrower margins and spaces around it, rather than by quotation marks. The name of the author should appear at the bottom of the material.

> there are two places in your paper where you recognize the work of others: the bibliography, and the footnote. The bibliography appears at the end of the paper. Footnotes, which are also called "attributions," appear in the body of your paper, in all of the places where outside material is used.

> "Attribution" separates your work from someone else's and recognizes the work of the other person (Rothman & Kolko, 2004).

International Students Ought to Know:

71.   that **a bibliography is a list of all of the resources you used in gathering information**, generally the last page of a paper, and can be used to look up more detailed information about sources you footnoted.

Bibliographies are usually arranged in alphabetical order by author's last name. They may also be grouped by subject, by date, or by another reasonable system. You should include: author(s), date of publication, title, edition, place of publication, and name of publisher. Consult a resource book for the correct form to use for items in your bibliography. A bibliographic entry for this book would read:

Rothman, J. & Kolko, S. (2004) <u>100 Things Every International Student Ought to Know, 1<u>st</u> Ed.</u> Williamsville, NY: Cambridge Stratford Ltd.

International Students Ought to Know:

72.   that **you may ask for help in writing a paper if you have difficulty with English**. Help should be related only to English language use and not to content, research, readings, or other work, which your professor expects you to do. Anything beyond English usage help will leave you open to possible questions about originality and cheating.

As you begin your semester's work, meet with your instructor(s) and let them know you aren't comfortable with English, and explain what kind of help you'll be using. Most instructors will be comfortable with this; however, **be sure to retain your own original work with the English errors in case the professor asks to see it**, as evidence that the work was your own.

If you plan to use this kind of help, you must begin your work earlier, so that the reader/tutor can have time to review and revise your work.

International Students Ought to Know:

73.   that **your adviser can help you explore your interests and abilities and plan your course of studies**. You can take special aptitude and interest tests, generally free of charge, to help you define your strengths, abilities and interests.

Another approach is to take courses that you think might be interesting, or in subjects you know little about, just to open up the possibilities and explore different fields of study, or to broaden your education. After you have chosen a major, taking elective courses in unrelated subjects increases your exposure to other fields of knowledge. The trick is to balance depth of knowledge in your chosen field with breadth of knowledge in many fields.

International Students Ought to Know:

74.   that **there are five good ways (at least) to learn how to use the library**, and you will probably use all of them at some time.

1)   Take a guided tour, offered by librarians, to learn about the main library systems, how to access information, and where to go with questions. This is an **excellent** resource.

2)   Look for literature near the information desk to help to guide you through the process of using the library and accessing information.

3) Librarians and librarian assistants will answer your questions and point you in the right direction.
4) Use the library's website to learn how to access catalogues, articles and journals, and other media in your library.
5) Use the "Help" on the library's website to assist you to use online resources.

International Students Ought to Know:

75.   that **personal problems can interfere with your studies**. If this is happening to you, use campus directories to access health and mental health services, and go to your school's Counseling Services. Your academic adviser, international student adviser, mentor, or tutor can help you locate services too, and may even contact the services and make an appointment for you Be careful about the kinds of personal issues you confide to anyone but a school counselor.

Before sharing personal information, ask the person you are talking with about confidentiality and limits. If you would like, ask that the information you share be kept private. Generally, confidentiality applies only to health and mental health professionals, and may be suspended if you share information which suggests that you are at risk of harm to yourself or to others.

Discussing Personal Matters

Student 1:   "What is your policy on confidentiality
regarding personal matters we discuss?"

Student 2:   "I pretend I'm not listening, just overhearing.
Then it's only hearsay. I'll never tell a soul."

3 Understanding the Turf and Your Place in It

International Students Ought to Know:

76.   that when you first meet people **they might ask what you "do."** One of the primary ways people are placed in society in the United States involves what career or employment or skill they may have which identifies them in some way. Because the United States is a nation of immigrants, because there is a high value placed on work and independence, because skills and education and interests vary widely, jobs and careers assume a very important role in the social order. People ask that question to get to know you and to begin a conversation and you shouldn't consider it rude or an invasion of privacy.

International Students Ought to Know:

77.   that the **US is a secular country**, and that "separation of church and state" is a basic part of our Constitution, which also grants freedom of religious practice to all groups.

The vast majority of the population in the United States practices Christianity. The largest religious group is Protestant, followed by Roman Catholics. There are relatively small minorities of other religious groups, such as Buddhists, Hindus, Jews, Moslems, Sikhs, and just about every religion in the world can claim adherents in the United States.

Because of the predominance of Christians, Christian holidays and traditions are widely practiced and accepted. However, any and all religious groups have the right to practice their religion in the United States.

International Students Ought to Know:

78.   that you can **locate religious organizations**, using the Yellow Pages telephone directory under "Churches," "Synagogues," "Mosques," and "Temples."

International Students Ought to Know:

79.   that **immigrants to the United States come from two very different social classes**. Some are professional and/or have special skills which are needed in the United States, computer and communications industry training, or are wealthy political exiles. This group of immigrants' experiences may be similar to your own in terms of their welcome.

Other immigrants may have left their countries for economic or political reasons, and come to the United States seeking a "better life." They do not know English, as you might, but must learn upon arrival. Because of the way in which society is organized in the United States, new immigrants are often at the very bottom of the social scale. They have unskilled labor or service jobs. They may be viewed as unwelcome strangers, and the period of acculturation may be long and difficult.

International Students Ought to Know:

80.   that you **CAN be held accountable for things you do not know**, ranging from laws to regulations to school policies. While knowledge is easily accessible, it can be quite challenging to figure out what it is that you need to know. The most important areas for you to learn about are related to driving, using credit cards, drinking alcohol, smoking marijuana, and cheating and plagiarism in written work.

One of the goals of this book is to provide you with some of this knowledge. Where do you find other knowledge? It is all around you! Online official government sites explain laws and policies, school sites tell you about courses and regulations and procedures, guides to cities and counties, shopping, product information—you can find just about everything you need to know. Your adviser, ISSO adviser, professors, friends, and classmates can also assist you, and there are on-campus events to help orient you to your new surroundings and to the expectations of school and society.

However, ultimately, the responsibility for acquiring the knowledge that you need is your own!

International Students Ought to Know:

81.   that in the US, **talking about race and dealing with issues about race is central to where we are at this time as a society**. Because of principles which guarantee equality, liberty, fair treatment, and justice to every person, issues which touch on the possibility of unfairness or less than equal treatment are very important.

Everyone, most especially college students, is very well aware of the conflicts and concerns which surround racial issues: discrimination, preferential policies such as affirmative action, distribution of national resources in education and healthcare, racial profiling—all of these are viewed not only as abstract concepts but also as racial issues. Positions on these and other issues are at the forefront of our national and political consciousness.

International Students Ought to Know:

82.   that **"hate crimes" are criminal actions** which are directed at individuals, property, institutions, or practices of a particular group of people *because* of membership in that group. Victims of hate crimes are primarily racial and religious minorities, and the crimes are often committed by members of organizations whose ideology include a mixture of belief in their own superiority and hatred of others. Groups such as the Ku Klux Klan and Aryan Nation are examples of organizations which perpetrate these kinds of crimes.

Hate crimes are prosecuted in courts of law, and there are a number of organizations that serve as "watchdogs" to warn potential victims, offer legal assistance, and gather evidence of such activity.

International Students Ought to Know:

83.   that **every city has public ordinances that govern expected behavior** in public spaces. There are statutes against loud noise levels (quiet times after certain hours, often 10 or 11 PM), "drunk and disorderly" behavior, "public exposure" (uncovering "private" body parts), crossing the street at corners rather than in the middle of the block ("jaywalking"), littering (throwing or leaving trash in public areas), sleeping in the streets or in parks or other public areas, urinating in the street, or in public, "panhandling" (approaching people to ask for money), cooking or setting up household in a public area not designated

for that purpose, and many others. The best way to find out about laws and ordinances in your area is to observe others' behavior and follow it. You may also find it helpful to discuss these issues with other students.

There are also laws which regulate parking, posted along streets. If rules about parking are not followed, you will receive a "parking ticket" which levies a fine. Your car may also be towed to another location, and high fees will be charged to you.

International Students Ought to Know:

84.   that if you are driving and **a police car pulls up behind you and flashes its lights, the officer wants you to "pull over," which means to stop your car at the side of the road**. Immediately move your car over to the right and look for a **safe** place to stop. If you are on a highway, the safe place will be to the right of the solid white line alone the right side of the road. If you are on a city street, a safe place will be against a curb. Do not get out of your car. The police officer will check your car's license against a database electronically, so it may take a few minutes for the officer to approach you. Stay in your car unless the police offer asks you to get out.

Give the officer your driver's license and your car's registration when asked for them. You will be told why you were stopped, and you may or may not have a brief conversation with the officer—this will vary from officer to officer and also with the nature of the reason you were asked to stop. The officer will go back to the police car with your license and registration, and check further with electronic databases. If there are no issues related to your license and registration, but only to your driving, your license and registration will be returned to you.

International Students Ought to Know:

85.   that **if you are stopped for a driving violation**, you will be given either

a **verbal warning** about your infraction,

a **written warning**, with no penalty fee required, or

a **"ticket"** which details your infraction and may or may not state the penalty fee.

Do not argue with the officer. Simply accept the ticket, and sign that you have received it if so requested. You are only

signing acknowledgment of receipt of the ticket and not admitting any guilt.

If you agree that you have committed a traffic violation, follow the directions and mail in the ticket and penalty. If you do not, follow the directions for requesting a court hearing. The officer will appear in court to present evidence of your violation and you may offer your defense.

International Students Ought to Know:

86.　　that **you have many rights as a non-citizen**. These include:

　　a.　You have right to remain silent—not to answer questions asked by a government agent.　However, you may be regarded suspiciously if you refuse.　You have the right to request to talk with a lawyer before answering any questions.　Anything that you say can be held against you, and you need to be aware that lying to the government is a criminal offense.

　　b.　The right not to have yourself, your home,　or your belongings searched or seized unless the agents have a warrant (an official legal permission to do so).　You can ask to see the warrant before any search. You do not have to answer any questions, however.

c. The right to peacefully ask for your rights or to protest government policies or actions. However, you should be aware that the INS can target you for deportation if you engage in these activities and **do not have a legal and valid visa to be in the United States**.

d. If you are arrested by the INS or other government agency, you have the right to remain silent and to request to contact a lawyer. You have the right to call your consulate and you should request to do so.

e. You have the right to be treated with respect by officers of the law. If you believe you are not being treated well, write down the officer's name, badge number, and any other information. Officers are required to give you their names and numbers. (ACLU, *Know Your Rights: What to Do if You're Stopped by the Police, the FBI, the INS, or other Customs Service* NY:Author)

f. If you believe you have been a victim of racial profiling - of being stopped, searched, refused a service, mistreated, or otherwise singled out for unusual treatment, you should contact the ACLU at 1-877-6-PROFILE.

International Students Ought to Know:

87.   that **US Customs officers may search you and/or your belongings when you enter the United States** in order to prevent the entry of illegal materials like drugs and weapons. Customs officers have the right to search everyone—citizens and non-citizens.

When you buy a ticket for air travel, you are giving permission for government authorities to scan your luggage and to search you and/or your belongings before you get on an airplane. It has not been legally determined whether you can avoid searches by agreeing not to fly and leaving the airport. The airplane's pilot has the right to refuse to fly a passenger he or she believes poses a threat to the safety of the airplane as a whole. Pilots must support their decisions. Racial profiling may not be used to determine whether a passenger poses a security risk.

Security procedures at borders, airports, ports and other travel facilities have become much tighter since the terrorist attacks of 9/11/2001.

International Students Ought to Know:

88.   that you should **carry proper identification** with you at all times. This includes your visa, student ID card, and other papers attesting to your identity and your legal status in the United States.

Photocopy originals of all identification and place the copies in a safe place to assist you if documents are lost or stolen. If this happens, you will need to contact:

a. your ISSO to help with forms and documentation,
b. the INS if your visa or other documents are lost or stolen, or
c. your school's security office or other school office if your school ID card is lost or stolen.

International Students Ought to Know:

89.   you have the **right to peaceably join in protests or political demonstrations**. If you become involved in violent or criminal activities such as defacing or destroying property or public buildings, you may be subject to fines and/or imprisonment, similar to any US citizen or resident. If you engage in demonstrations and your visa is expired, or you do not have proper legal documentation, you could be asked to leave the country.

If you choose to participate in demonstrations, always have your identification with you!

International Students Ought to Know:

90.   that state governments grant driver's licenses and car registrations, and that the procedures vary by state. To obtain a driver's license or register a car, you should contact your state's Motor Vehicle Administration (MVA) or Department of Motor Vehicles (DMV).

You must inform the DMV of any change in address and keep their records current. If you miss a license renewal or a registration renewal because the information has gone to an incorrect address, you will be responsible for fees and penalties.

International Students Ought to Know:

91.   to **get a driver's license you will need**:
   a.   a completed application form,
   b.   your valid passport and documentation, and
   c.   a passing grade on a written test of motor vehicle laws
and regulations. The DMV will have all of this information
available to you in a booklet and you may study the booklet for
as long as necessary.
   d.   A passing grade on a "road test" of your driving. Road
tests may be given on city streets or in special areas of the DMV.

You will be asked to park, back up, and follow other directions by your examiner.

    e.   A passing grade on an eye examination, given at the DMV, which attests that you see well both at night and during the day. Your vision may be corrected with glasses or contact lenses, and this restriction will be noted on your license.

    f.   A fee.

You will be notified by mail when you must renew your license.

International Students Ought to Know:

92.   to **register a car you will need**:

a. a completed application form,

b. a certificate that attests to your car's level of emissions (gases that are passed into the air through your car's tailpipe, which you must obtain from a "smog-check" gas station. The gas station is entitled to charge a fee for this service.),

c. a car inspection which is done at the DMV, et. al.

d. a fee, and

e. proof of insurance coverage for your vehicle.

You will then be given license plates and your car's registration. You should affix the license plates immediately, and always keep your car's registration in the glove compartment for easy availability.

Registrations are often renewed annually, and a fee must be paid each year. Smog checks must also be repeated according to your state's schedule. You will receive renewal information by mail.

International Students Ought to Know:

93.   that you should **inspect any apartment** you will be renting for damages before you rent it, and note damages in writing on the rental agreement or contract you are asked to sign. (see below). You will be asked for a "deposit"—generally two months' rent. Your deposit covers money to repair any damages you cause to the apartment. If the cost of the damages is more than the deposit, the rental agent can ask you for additional money for repairs, and can sue you if you refuse to pay. If you leave the apartment in the same condition in which you received it, the full amount of your deposit will be returned to you.

You can rent a furnished (with furniture, kitchenware, etc.) or unfurnished apartment. If your apartment is rented furnished, leave all furniture there when you leave, and keep it in the condition in which it was rented to you. Normal "wear and tear" is acceptable. You can have anyone live with you in your apartment, unless the rental contract limits this. You must comply with local rules about numbers of people per housing unit, noise, outside clutter, etc.

International Students Ought to Know:

94.   that a **contract is a binding legal agreement** between two parties about what may or may not occur between them in a specified circumstance, and you should be very careful about understanding all the terms and conditions. Rental agreements are contracts, as a health club memberships, car loan agreements, and credit cards. Contracts specify *who* will do *what* under *which* conditions.

Read contracts carefully, consult with someone to be sure you understand completely, and don't agree to terms you can't fulfill. Buying a car without the money for the monthly payments, charging things on a credit card without the funds to pay for them, joining a club with the intent of not paying for membership—all of these can create serious legal problems for you!

Both parties to the contract have the legal right to enforce the terms and conditions each has agreed to. If the rental agent has agreed to paint the apartment for you by a specific date, and does not, he or she is in violation, and is legally liable in the same way that you would be if you did not pay your rent when it was due.

International Students Ought to Know:

95.   that when **either party does not meet the terms of a contract, the other party can bring the issue to the court system**. These kinds of lawsuits are civil—that is, they are generally not crimes, like assault and battery (attacking and beating another person), car theft, or murder—and they carry penalties which do not often involve time in prison. Most civil lawsuits will require that the grievances by addressed, often with monetary penalties added.

If you are sued for not meeting the terms of a contract you have signed ("breach of contract") it is best to consult with a lawyer who is familiar with American legal processes.

International Students Ought to Know:

96.   that **before joining a gym, you should consider**:
a. cost - prices vary,
b. location,
c. classes offered and equipment available, and
d. services available.

A gym membership is a legal contract. Commonly, you will pay an initial fee, and then a monthly fee. You can extend your membership annually with no further initial fees. Your monthly fee can be withdrawn directly from your bank account, or automatically billed to your credit card. You are obligated to pay your fee for the entire term of the contract whether or not you use the gym, but you can bargain with the gym about terms and fees. If you want to terminate your membership after the initial contract period, **you must notify the gym in writing**. If you return home for a period of time, your monthly fees might be suspended—check with your gym.

You may be a member of more than one gym if you like.

International Students Ought to Know:

97.   that **if you go to a healthcare facility which is not a part of your school's health plan, you will be personally responsible for any bills** you may incur. American medical care is very expensive, so it is important to be careful!

If you need medical attention, you must first contact your school health service, and follow their instructions. In the case of non-emergency care, you will be offered an appointment during clinic hours at the health service. In case of emergency, they will direct you to go to a specific facility with which the school has arrangements for your care. Keep the school's health service phone number handy, and use it as needed!

International Students Ought to Know:

98.   that the **health coverage you purchase as a part of your educational package is usually limited**, and may not give you the emergency coverage you need when you are living abroad. It may only cover your needs for routine medical and psychological services. Your family's medical insurance may not be accepted in the United States, and it may be difficult for you to arrange to be reimbursed for expenses you have incurred outside of your own country.

There are a number of insurance companies that specialize in working with international students and scholars. These specialize in emergency and accidental health coverage and are excellent supplements to your school's health plan. They include:

Scholastic Overseas Services	1-800-767-1403	internationalsos.com
HTH Worldwide Insurance Services	1-800-242-4178	hthstudents.com
TW Lord Associates	1-800-633-2360	twlord.com
The Harbour Group	1-800-252-8160	hginsurance.com
International Student Organization	1-800-244-1180	isoa.org

International Students Ought to Know:

99.   that it's **not unusual for international students to feel anxious and depressed**. Immersing yourself in another culture, learning and using another language, finding your way around a new city, dealing with courses and assignments in a language not your own, making new friends, and being far from home and loved ones is difficult! Adjusting to school is stressful for everyone, and much more so when culture shock is added to the mixture!

It is not considered a sign of mental illness, weakness, or deficiency in the United States to ask for help with depression and anxiety. If you feel anxious or depressed, contact your school's counseling service. The counselors you will be working with are experienced and have helped many students with these issues. If you are having trouble getting the help you need at school, ask for a community referral.

International Students Ought to Know:

100.   that **personal health and mental health records in the US must be kept confidential** by law. The only exceptions are: where information is needed by your insurance company to reimburse your health provider, or when sharing information is essential to your own health and care. If you need to be referred to a specialist or other healthcare provider, you will be offered the choice to refuse such a referral. You family will not be contacted.

You can go outside the school's health services system to a local health care provider and pay privately for your consultation or care if you wish. Large cities also have low cost public health clinics which offer privacy from the school's system.

The only exception that may be made in contacting your family without your prior knowledge and consent involves life-threatening emergencies, such as a suicide attempt or an illness or accident where you are at risk of major harm or death or are unable to give consent. In such cases, if you are under age 21, your family may be contacted.

International Students Ought to Know:

101.   the **differences between the two broad categories of medicines** in the US: prescription drugs and "over-the-counter" (OTC) medications.

Prescription medicines must be "prescribed" by your physician for a condition or illness for which you are being treated by that physician. Certain classes of medicines, such as narcotics, are available only by prescription. You can get prescribed medicines in two ways: you may be given a paper (with the physician's identifying information on it) which you may take to a pharmacy and fill; or your prescription may be "called in" by your physician's office to the pharmacy you choose. You then pick the medication up from the pharmacy.

OTC medicines may be purchased without prescription and are available on open shelves in drug stores, supermarkets, and pharmacies. They include remedies for common ailments, such as coughs or colds, joint and muscle pain, gas or stomach acidity, constipation and diarrhea, and sleeplessness. Be sure to read the directions carefully for any OTC: they can have a powerful effect even if they are "over-the-counter!"

International Students Ought to Know:

102. the **difference between a pharmacy and a drug store**.   Pharmacies specialize only in medicines, both prescription and OTC, and often carry special medical equipment and supplies as well. Drug stores generally do not carry medical equipment or specialized supplies. They have a pharmacy located within the store to fill all prescriptions, and have a wide array of OTC's. Drug stores also carry toiletries, school supplies, some food and candy, some clothing, toys, and other necessaries. Pharmacies are also often located in supermarkets, with both prescription services and OTC's.

International Students Ought to Know:

103.   that one of the **best sources of information for price-shopping are your American classmates**, especially those who come from the city you are living in. They will know all the good places to shop. Some other suggestions:

General (clothing and household goods): outlet malls in your city (usually on the outskirts), and discount chains, such as Target, K-Mart or 99 cent Stores. Some discount chains, such as Costco or Sam's Club, require that you become a "member" for a small annual fee. Discount drug store chains have reasonable prices for household good, school supplies, and toiletries.

Retail stores have sales on a regular basis—watch newspapers for ads. They also have sale racks in almost every department. Merchandise on sale racks is in good condition—it may just be out of season. All clothing items will go on sale. If you purchase an item at the regular price, ask for the sale price adjustment policy and keep your receipt. If the item goes on sale within 14 days, take your receipt back for an adjustment. After 14 days, you may not be given an adjustment.

Furniture and Kitchenware: Reasonably priced new furniture and kitchenware can be found at Pier One or Cost Plus.

Food: Good values for food can be found at outdoor fresh produce markets and discount supermarket chains.

School Supplies: You may find good prices for textbooks and other things online. Amazon.com has a used book department, which offers textbooks at highly discounted rates.

Tickets for shows and events: Most major cities have a same-day ticket outlet where tickets may be purchased at half price.

International Students Ought to Know:

104.   in general, **the US is not a bargaining society**. Exceptions include outdoor markets, flea markets, trade shows, or garage sales, where bargaining is expected. Sales clerks cannot bargain or make price adjustments and you should not ask this of them. Most items you purchase will not be open for bargaining. Shops in malls, grocery stores, gas stations, office supply stores, movie and theater tickets, and restaurants have non-negotiable written prices. You can ask if the items will be going on sale, or if there are any specials. More expensive items ("big-

ticket" items) like cars, homes, businesses, gym memberships, travel, high-end furniture and rugs may be bargained for. You may also bargain for warranties and service contracts.

Trading and bartering for goods is also rare in the US. Trades and barter are legally taxable on the value obtained. Evading taxes on traded items is a legal offense.

International Students Ought to Know:

105.   that each merchant is responsible for **collecting taxes on items sold**, and must keep careful records of taxes collected. The US does not have a VAT (value added tax) similar to that of many European nations. Taxes on items purchased are regulated by the states, and are used as revenue for public services. Therefore, the amount of taxes, and the items that are taxable, will vary by state. Some major cities, such as New York, have an additional tax levied by the city.

Almost everything can be taxable. The most common taxable items are: clothing, household goods, toiletries, furniture, cars, appliances, electronic items, books, jewelry, cameras, etc. Food eaten in restaurants is generally taxed, although many states do not charge if the food is taken out to be consumed outside of the premises. Some states do not tax "essential" items like clothing. Food items purchased at grocery or other shops are generally not taxed, but non-food items purchased in these same stores are taxed.

International Students Ought to Know:

106.   The **Internet is the best resource for travel information**. Just type in where you want to go, and select activities, accommodations, or restaurants to view a wide selection of possibilities.   Large universities also have travel agencies on campus which specialize in budget travel for students. For airplane tickets and other travel you can contact Orbitz, CheapTickets, Expedia, Travelocity, and Travelzoo by telephone or online. Budget travel guides, such as Arthur Frommer's books, the Lonely Planet series, and budget travel magazines are available in your campus bookstore.

The National Park Service has inexpensive places to stay in many national parks: cabins and tents can be reserved online, or are available on a walk-in basis. YMCA's and YWCA's in major cities offer inexpensive rooms and meals for budget travelers. The cheapest way to travel and stay is to use AYC 's (American Youth Hostel) network of residences throughout the United States. If you are a member of your country's hostel organization, you may use facilities in the United States as well.

International Students Ought to Know:

107. you **can use the Internet to order products from your country** which are not readily available in your location. The availability of food, cosmetics, clothing and other items from foreign countries will vary according to the country and the location from which you are seeking them. Products tend to be available where there is a demand for them, so you will most easily find them in ethnic communities: Chinese in Chinatowns, Korean in Koreatowns, Russian in Orthodox neighborhoods, Italian in Little Italys, etc. Grocery stores throughout the country also carry many international food products, and have sections for ethic foods.

Department Store Conversations

Student: "You say I owe you $179.54 for these items plus $13.47 in sales tax and you won't accept this handmade jewelry and my offer to work for you for two full days. Well, what would you say if I said, 'Keep your items?'"

Store Clerk: "Next in line please!"

4 Interacting with Friends Safely/Legally

International Students Ought to Know:

108. that **if you live in international student housing, you'll have other international students for support and advice**, who may speak your language, and share your culture, foods, values, and activities. You will have easier and more immediate access to support services, and may have built-in connections to community groups from your culture.

But, is being with people from your own culture the reason you're studying in the US? Living with American students helps develop friendships, and gives you daily opportunities to experience the culture and to practice English. You'll be in easier touch with things going on around campus, and be able to ask for advice from people who know the culture and rules.

International Students Ought to Know:

109. that **not all campuses have a large group of international students**. If yours does not, you may find yourself wishing you could talk with someone who understands your culture shock and your problems as an international student. You don't have to feel alone—you can go online! There are chat groups for international students and an international students community at groups.msn.com/InternationalStudentsinUS. There's also an International Student Exchange and Study Abroad Resource Center with forums for students at Abroadplanet.com. There are international student communities at community.abroadplanet.com.

International Students Ought to Know:

110. that **the best places to meet people are: in classes, at meals, in the library, in coffee shops, at concerts and campus events, and at activities**. You'll find that most people are friendly and outgoing and ready to be friends. It's fine to start a conversation with other students, to suggest going for coffee, to a party, or to a campus event, or to study together.

A lot of socializing in the US happens around food, so campus eating places and coffee shops are especially good places to meet people.

International Students Ought to Know:

111. that **posters, handouts, school newspapers, book-lets, organization and activity fairs on campus, and the Internet are good places to learn about on-campus organizations, clubs and events that might interest you**. You can also check department offices for information about organizations linked to them, such as an astronomy club, a drama club, or the school orchestra.

If you like sports—both spectator and participatory, you can try out for team sports, or play in informal leagues and clubs. Major campus events such as football and basketball games are great places to meet people and get into the "school spirit!"

International Students Ought to Know:

112. that **men and women are viewed as equal** intellectually, financially, socially, legally, and academically. Because this has only been true for the past 50 years, you'll see traces of earlier social norms and customs. For example, it is customary for men to pay for dinner on a first date, even though equality demands that each pay half. A woman may ask to split the bill, or to pay, but if a man wants to show he's interested, he'll pay the full bill. After the first few dates, these matters become more equal. Men are still expected to begin calling and contacting women if they are interested in dating. If you are a woman, you should feel comfortable in calling a man—after he has indicated interest in you!

International Students Ought to Know:

113.   that **relationships between the sexes are casual in dorms**, especially in co-ed dorms. People of both sexes are often out in the hall in a bathrobe, without shoes on, or scantily dressed, and visit each other in their rooms. Close friends of the opposite sex may hug, hold hands, or otherwise display affection—it doesn't mean there's a romantic relationship. In same-sex relationships with no romantic interests, women can exchange hugs or kisses upon meeting, but don't usually hold hands or walk with their arms around each other. Men generally do not display affection toward other men by hugging or kissing in the United States. Older people are treated less casually—as they are in all cultures.

International Students Ought to Know:

114. that **gangs are groups of people who share identities, interests, and purposes**, whose members are often inner city minority young people. Gangs provide support, socialization, and identification for members, but many gangs are also involved in violent and/or illegal activities, drug and alcohol use, and anti-social behavior. Gangs usually have elaborate, secret, and violent initiation rituals, require complete allegiance and loyalty, have a distinct public image, display logos and emblems and wear certain colors, and do not easily let people leave the group once initiated and accepted.

Because of the criminal, violent, and anti-social behavior of most gangs, and the difficulties of dis-joining should one wish to do so, joining a gang is not advisable. Association with criminal behavior will affect your standing at school and your visa, which may be revoked. You can also be expelled from the US by being involved with illegal or criminal gang activities.

International Students Ought to Know:

115. that **if you don't make friends with American students, you'll really limit your chances to learn about American culture**. Though it may be difficult at first, you'll find that American students will welcome you, and will be interested in learning about your country, culture, and language. It's just as much a vital part of *their* learning experience to learn about *you*.

One of the most important pieces of your study in the US comes from outside of the classroom—in the direct contact that you have with fellow students. Don't waste them! Set a goal for yourself: at least one American friend from each class! Think about the goals you have for yourself as an international student. Do you just want to get your degree and go home? Or are you interested in broadening your views and have different kinds of life experiences? You can easily do both!

International Students Ought to Know:

116.   that even though it's difficult and somewhat annoying to have to keep explaining about your culture, traditions, national structures and values, and other things to people over and over, **every person who travels abroad is their country's "good will ambassador"**—they represent their country to the people they are meeting. You may be the only person they will meet from your country, and what you say and how you act will forever be their image of your country.

Yes, you may have to do some repeating! You can help yourself by having some literature from your country's Tourist Office or other government office to give people for answers to some of their questions.

International Students Ought to Know:

117. that, although disagreement and discourse is encouraged on all campuses, there may be times, particularly when world events affect your part of the world, that **you and American students will disagree** regarding things like the environment, the use of global resources, political systems of government, wars, internal events, economic policies, etc. If you know yours is a minority opinion, or you are concerned that it will

insult or anger American students, you may feel uncomfortable expressing it, and feel frustrated and upset.

You may find it is easier to begin this "conversation" in a classroom, forum, or conference, or with a group of students from your country. School newspapers, radio stations, and the Internet are places that can provide a way for your ideas and opinions to be heard.

International Students Ought to Know:

118. that **harassment can include ridicule, taunts, negative comments, unwanted attention, withdrawal, isolation, and ostracism**. Harassment is defined culturally and may be quite different in the US than it is in your country.

If you feel you're being harassed or threatened, there are special faculty, staff, and support services on every campus skilled in helping you with this. Generally, you will be asked to meet with the student(s) in a supported and structured environment, and the school will arrange greater opportunities for dialogue and support, as well as providing guidance to the student body as a whole about respect for other viewpoints.

International Students Ought to Know:

119.   that **"hyphenated Americans" still see themselves as affiliated with your country, but they are really very different from you or other people from your country**. Even though they may share your language, traditions, food, religious observances, family structures, etc., they have been very much affected by their immersion in American culture. So, Mexican-Americans differ from Mexicans, but also from the generic "American," as do Chinese-Americans, Nigerian-Americans, Peruvian-Americans, and Danish-Americans.

Their "culture" is a unique blend of elements of both cultures. Some people are even unable to communicate completely in either of the cultural languages. "Spanglish" is a common term for the way in which people from Latin America who are also Americans may speak.

Hyphenated Americans are eager to have contact with people from their country of origin, but, unless they have visited your country, you'll need to help them understand the way your country is today.

International Students Ought to Know:

120. that **some of your new American friends may want to come and visit you in your country**.   You can help them to plan their visit by telling them about your country and culture, and by giving them material to read. If the social mores and customs of dress and social interaction are very different in your country, you need to help your friends to be prepared.

You will probably want to host your friends in your home at least part of the time. It might be helpful to prepare your family, and to share with them some of the social norms and customs of the US so that they will be comfortable with your guests.

International Students Ought to Know:

121. that **first dates are often a movie, dinner, attendance at a special event, a sporting event, or a lecture**. You'll be spending some time alone with the person, getting to know each other. Be prepared to share something about yourself and your life; you don't need to share any personal business such as finances, family relationships, or sexual issues. Keep your personal information personal until you have developed enough of a relationship to know you can trust your date. Some easy things to talk about on a first date: school and courses you are taking, events you have attended, and some information about your country.

International Students Ought to Know:

122. that **intimacy is a complex tangle of degrees of contact, emotion, and tradition or social norms**. Holding hands, kissing, walking closely together mean different things in different cultures. Always be sure that you are comfortable and agree with any intimate contact—there are enormous variations in sexual mores in this country , in spite of what you may see on TV and in the movies!

You may or may not find yourself dealing with issues of intimacy on a first date. Be careful not to become involved too quickly in things that aren't comfortable. Being asked on a date does not carry an obligation of physical intimacy. Paying for dinner is not a ticket for physical contact or for sex. If you do want to have physical contact, be sure that the desire is mutual before becoming involved.

International Students Ought to Know:

123. that **it's customary to date more than one person at a time**. However, if you are on your third or fourth date, you may want to discuss the nature of your relationship and your feelings for the other person to be sure there is a mutual understanding. If you are dating more than one person, it is courteous and appropriate for you to let the other person know at that point. If you are having sexual relations, you may decide to date that person exclusively.

International Students Ought to Know:

124. that **"living together" does not necessarily mean there is a romantic interest or a sexual interest involved**. It is not at all uncommon for people of opposite sexes to share an apartment or house. You may want to live together because you are good friends, or because it is convenient, or because you feel safe and secure with the person. The relationship may not involve any intimacy, but only a shared responsibility for rent and upkeep of your common living quarters.

On the other hand, you may be dating someone and/or be having a sexual relationship which involves so much time and energy that it seems to make sense to share a living space. You may want to "try out" living with someone to see if your relationship works well at that level of intimacy as a prelude to long-term commitment or marriage.

International Students Ought to Know:

125. that **living together with someone in a romantic relationship may limit your options for dating and meeting other people**. People will generally avoid getting involved with someone who they see as already committed to another person. If you are not sure about the person you would be living with as a long-term relationship, it might be better to live separately. If you are having a relationship but are not living with the other person, there will still be opportunities for meeting other people.

You should not be preoccupied with what your fellow students think, although you may welcome their input and advice. The decision about living with someone in a romantic relationship is yours alone.

International Students Ought to Know:

126.   if **the INS suspects that you have married a US citizen only or primarily to become a citizen, they will take steps to block the citizenship process**. Criteria they will use include: cohabitation—that is, whether a couple is living together; and consummation—whether a couple has had sexual relations. Compensation, financial or otherwise, given to the US citizen spouse may also be used as evidence. INS service agents can visit you at home or make inquiries to determine if your marriage has met these criteria.

If you want to become a US citizen, there are other, less risky ways to do it. Ask your employer for help, participate in the lottery, or get on the waiting list for citizenship through the US embassy in your country. You may also elect a career path which is given preferential consideration.

International Students Ought to Know:

127. that **your feelings about marrying a person selected by your family may change**, and letting your family know you want to choose your mate independently will be a challenge. This issue affects a broad group of international students and may be addressed both formally and informally by cultural organizations and the ISSO on your campus. The more your family visits you, the more you share with them what you are learning and your life experiences in the United States, the

greater will be the chances that they will understand and/or accept your feelings. After all, they agreed to your attending school in the US!

As you think through this important issue, don't assume that you will decide against the traditional ways. Think carefully and reasonably and you may be quite surprised at what you finally decide!

International Students Ought to Know:

128.   that **there's a blue light system on most large campuses for emergencies**. Blue lights which are lit up at night are next to telephones and hotlines where you may access instant assistance in the event of an emergency. You don't need coins to use blue light phones.

Walk around campus and notice where all the blue lights are. At night, use walkways and areas where blue lights are easily accessible. In the event of an emergency, activate the system and assistance will arrive quickly.

Campus Security/ Campus Police are first responders to the blue light system.

There are fines and penalties for misuse of the system, for defacing it, or for rendering it ineffective.

International Students Ought to Know:

129. that even though campuses are generally safe at night, **be careful**! Some ideas that will help:

a. Large campuses have "night routes," clearly marked on placards around campus and in booklets from Campus Security. These are the most used, best lit, and most heavily patrolled routes. Use them even if they're a little out of your way.

b. Use the campus transit system for long distances. Bus stops are well lit and near blue light stations.

c.   Walk in pairs or groups for safety.
d.   Let someone know where you are going so that if you
     don't arrive in a reasonable time, help can be contacted.
e.   Most large campuses have escort services: volunteers, usu-
     ally male students, who will walk you back to your dorm
     or other location at night. Escort service numbers are on
     campus map placards, and are listed in campus informa-
     tion. Keep the number handy!

International Students Ought to Know:

130.   to **contact Campus Security or the local police department to find out what areas of the city are safe**. There is often a day/night difference in safety of certain areas. It is always best to visit a new or unknown area of the city by day, in the company of others if possible!

International Students Ought to Know:

131. to **immediately contact the police (campus or city) if you are raped, mugged, or attacked**. Give a report and go to the police station to be interviewed if you're asked to do so. If you have been raped or physically harmed, ask to be taken to a hospital emergency room for an examination. If you have been raped, be sure to ask for an advocate from the local Rape Crisis Center to accompany you to the hospital. Have this person in the room with you during your medical examination.

Ask that a friend be contacted and have them accompany you home. Follow any medical instructions carefully and attend follow-up appointments.

International Students Ought to Know:

132.   that **being a victim of a violent crime is very traumatic**. Talking about it with friends can help, but may not be enough.   Contact your school's counseling service, support groups, hotlines, and medical services to help you to deal with the experience.   The sooner you call them, the faster you'll get the help you need.

You may be asked to testify or to appear in court in order to bring the perpetrator to justice if he or she is caught.   It's your right to refuse; however, you will be leaving the perpetrator free to inflict harm again and to victimize another person.

International Students Ought to Know:

133. that in the US, **you need a permit to carry arms**, and these generally need to be visible and not hidden under clothing or other objects. People don't carry guns unless they are hunting or target-shooting, or are an officer of the law. Knives are less strongly legislated, and it is OK to carry a jackknife or other small knife. There are many kinds of "tear gasses"—their legality varies by state. Pepper spray is generally acceptable to carry and use, mace is not. Call the local police department before buying any arms to find out about laws in your state.

Remember, in an emergency, your protection can be used against you, or may incite your attacker to further violence.

International Students Ought to Know:

134. that **some kinds of foods and drugs may not be sold or distributed in the US**. Others are "controlled"— they can be sold or distributed only by licensed physicians or druggists. Narcotics and opiates are examples of "controlled" substances.

The Food and Drug administration is responsible for reviewing all food, drink, and medications in this country to ensure that consuming them is safe.

International Students Ought to Know:

135. that **you can bring your medications into the US**. However, it's not wise to bring in a medication that's not approved for use in the US: you will be carrying an illegal substance and can be detained or fined. Also, US physicians may not understand side effects and potential problems you may experience, and you will be unable to get refills.

Consult your physician before you leave your country and obtain an alternative medication!

International Students Ought to Know:

136. that **marijuana and all "street drugs" such as heroin, PCP, ecstasy, and cocaine are banned substances** in the United States.

International Students Ought to Know:

137. if **you are caught smoking or distributing marijuana, you will be arrested and charged**. You may be detained at a police station or you may be released under a "bail bond." If you are caught *distributing* marijuana or other controlled or banned substances, a much more serious circumstance, you will be given a jury trial. You should immediately get a lawyer, either privately or through the Office of the Public Defender.

International Students Ought to Know:

138. If **you are caught using or distributing banned or controlled substances in the United States you may be sent to jail, your visa may be revoked, you may be dismissed from school, and you may be asked to leave the country when your jail sentence is completed**.

International Students Ought to Know:

139. that **a bail bond is a guarantee which you give to the court that you will not leave the area until your case comes to trial**. Bail bonds are sums of money set by a judge which are held by the court. They are returned to you when you appear for trial. If you or your family do not have the money to post a bail bond, there are professional bail bond offices which will lend you the money and charge for their services.

If you do not appear in court, the money is forfeited and both the justice system and the bail bond company will try to find you.

International Students Ought to Know:

140. that a person **under 21 years of age is a minor** in most states and may not consume alcohol.

International Students Ought to Know:

141. that **"dry" campuses do not permit alcohol** anywhere on campus properties. In most states, the "legal" age for drinking alcohol is 21. Younger people are not permitted to consume alcohol. Campuses which are not "dry" ("wet" campuses) allow only students over 21 to drink alcohol on campus. "Dry" campuses exclude all alcohol consumption no matter what age you are.

If you wish to drink alcohol and are over 21 and on a "dry" campus, you can go off-campus. If you are under 21, you can't legally consume alcoholic beverages anywhere in most states.

International Students Ought to Know:

142. that **if you're having a problem controlling your use of drugs or alcohol, you should go to your school's health services, or counseling services, or call their hotline**.   Your academic adviser or your international student adviser can also refer you for help.

If you don't want anyone at school to know about your problem, you can go to community mental health clinics, hospital clinics, or other resources. Check your city's yellow pages under "alcoholism," "social service and welfare organizations," and "hotlines." You can also ask a friend or fellow student for suggestions. Choose who you tell carefully: you want help, not reassurance that you don't have a problem, criticism, or judgment!

International Students Ought to Know:

143. that **people often make wrong assumptions about people from known drug-producing nations**. If this happens to you, use this opportunity to educate your friends about your country, some of the problems your country faces, and the efforts that are being made to address them. You will find that people are interested and receptive to this kind of information.

International Students Ought to Know:

144. that **you don't need to report another student or friend's drug use** to the police. Depending on the circumstances, you may want to encourage the person to get help.

International Students Ought to Know:

145. that if you are asked to appear in court and testify as to the actions and behavior of someone who is being tried for criminal activity of any kind including drug use **you must respond truthfully and honestly** or face penalties yourself which include the possible suspension of your student visa.

Conclusion

To the Reader

Writing this book has been like taking an around-the-world journey—and it's been a wonderful experience for us! We have talked with students from many countries, written down their suggestions and advice, sat in dorm rooms and cafes and lounges, listened in on conversations with Mom and Dad back home, and shared in whatever was going on at that very moment between and among people. We learned about the lives of wealthy students, and about the problems facing those on loans and scholarships. We learned about medical problems, problems with cars, international cell phones, African headgear, and the close relationship between the French House and the Spanish House. We learned about students who wanted to stay, those who wanted to play, and those whose commitment was primarily to their education. We learned about dating other international students, and about dating Americans.

We have come away from this experience with an abiding respect for each of you—for your enthusiasm, your interest in America, and the special things you each have brought with you from your country to share with us. New (to us) ideas and ways of doing things, new challenges to settled programs and thoughts help us all to grow and to gain a greater understanding of and appreciation for this world in which we all live.

We would like to ask a special favor of you. We would like you to share your thoughts about what we have included here, and any ideas and suggestions for things we might want to add. We have included a simple form for you to use. If you prefer to remain anonymous, you do not need to fill in your name and address.

Appendix

Editorial Comments and Contribution Pages

Dear Reader,

Your comments can help other international students make a smoother transition to college. Please share your thoughts, ideas, and suggestions on the following pages or on a separate sheet of paper. Also, fill in the biographical information below. We'll include a special reference by-line in my next edition to acknowledge all contributors. Thank you!

Name		☐ *Student*
		☐ *Faculty*
Institution		☐ *Administrator*
		☐ *Family/Friend*
City	State ___ Zip ___	☐ _____

(Cut or tear out form or e-mail to Cambridges@aol.com)

My thoughts, ideas, and suggestions are

_____

_____

_____

_____

_____

_____

_____

_____

_____

_____

_____

(Cut or tear out form or e-mail to Cambridges@aol.com)

_____

_____

_____

_____

_____

_____

_____

_____

Mail To: Juliet C. Rothman and Susan R. Kolko
             c/o The Cambridge Stratford Study Skills Institute
             8560 Main Street
             Williamsville, NY 14221

(Cut or tear out form or e-mail to Cambridges@aol.com)

Student's Comments and Advice

The students with whom we spoke come from China, Hong Kong, Japan, Vietnam, Thailand, Korea, Malaysia, Fiji, Samoa, New Zealand, Peru, Brazil, Chile, Mexico, Canada, England, Finland, Sweden, France, Germany, Spain, Italy, Croatia, Dubai, United Arab Emirates, Israel, Egypt, Kenya, Namibia, Tasmania, India, Pakistan, and Nepal.

They attend school at Academy of Art College, American Intercontinental University, American University, Boston University, Boston College, Catholic University, Columbia University, Holy Names College, New York University, San Francisco State University, Santa Monica College, Syracuse University, Tufts University, University of California, Berkeley, University of California, Davis and Washington University

They especially wanted to share their own special thoughts and advice with you.

"I really needed help understanding about contracts. I wanted to rent an apartment and the manager gave me these pages and pages of legal material. Don't sign anything without understanding every single word!"

"After September 11th, situations about visas are changing rapidly. You need to keep up with all the new laws and changes!"

"Registration" and "enrolling" are different. Such complicated procedures can be really confusing! Be sure you understand what each word means!"

"Services and procedures in daily life are so rough. It's important to take the time to know the quality, delays, and misunderstandings ahead of time!"

"It's really important to know about health and accident insurance. The insurance that you get from my country doesn't cover any health problems due to pregnancy. It's very important to check this if you're coming to the US."

"With the INS, if you do any activities that you get as school credit, like a paid internship, you have to fill out paperwork! Don't just think because it's connected to a course it's OK to just do it!"

"Cultural differences are more than just statistics, it's about how does it feel. It's good to know the statistics, but also to talk about how you feel."

"I can't say enough about medical insurance - we really need to understand exactly what they cover."

"I am not only here to learn about classes, but also my surroundings. Try to learn about cultural activities where your university is."

"I have problems with no one knowing what the other person is doing, so I ask one place and they keep sending me around without knowing anything. After all this, I am to blame for not knowing what I have to do! Go to your ISSO office—that's the best place to go for help!"

"My university is actually very helpful about courses and registration and degrees and programs of study. I'm on my own about the other stuff, but I ask other international students."

"Although we, international students, know about our visa status, there are still many things we should know but we don't know. I guess it's because it's not easy to get that information. It is very important to know about visas!"

"Some people are racist and say stupid things. You can get very angry with this. Just don't pay attention and find friends who aren't racist."

"Even in my school, international students are treated so differently. We don't receive the same services as Americans. We have to know what the reason is—is it some legal problem or is it racism."

"Some instructors don't treat us equally. We all know that but why do they do that? The best way to find out is to talk to them. I have made very good friends with professors."

"Every university has its own books about academic success. I think it's important to know you can approach student instructors easily."

"There are so many cultures here at my University that there is not a particular culture or holiday. I don't find it important to follow one or the other. You may find that sometimes you are aware of your culture and other times you are not."

"Everything depends so much on your social surrounding here - friends and dating and sports and other activities. It's important to find other international students."

"I wish all the info on money, visa, degree topics could be explained more easily. It takes up so much time to learn all that. But you have to do it."

"I think the departments should try more for finding contacts for students for jobs and internships because contacts are so important in today's job search. It's hard for us to find contacts on our own. Don't be afraid to ask for help!"

"You need to understand about credit and "building credit" and how that works in the United States."

"Americans are so "me" focused—are individualistic vs. communal society. They don't share notes from class. It's a big cultural change for me. Be prepared!"

"Student-teacher relationships are different here. It is good to talk with your teachers."

"I want to know more about the state divisions and the federal government, representatives, and work permits. I think it's important and there are some good websites to help. Try your state, city, county— even the federal government!

"I really need insights about American way of life and college immersion! I get a lot of good information at orientation. Don't skip going to that!"

"I don't understand about finding a job if I'm not a US citizen. You can't just go out and get one—there are all kinds of restrictions. Ask at the International Student office."

"It is important to make the school and the professor understand that English is not your first language. Tell each one of your teachers and take an ESL course if you need it."

"Some things bother me. Some instructors would not consider the language problems we might have. Some people are racist. Some people are ignorant. I learned that I can't change all these things. I just try to be around people that are not like that."

© 2004 by Cambridge Stratford, LTD.

"We need to know about restrictions you might have because of university policy that you might not have back home. There are so many policies and rules. But it's our job to learn them all!"

"I think it's important for us to know all about the United States, the history, national holidays and values, culture and tradition. I'm an accounting major and it's hard to learn all that and accounting too. I learn a lot from being around American students—that's the easiest way."

"I think it's important to know more about resources in my school, and where to go for help. I made a list of important phone numbers and I carry it with me."

"I don't have a visa problem, but I worry about what I would do if I did have one. Check in with your International Program office regularly and always read all your mail from them so you don't miss anything."

"You are going to get homesick. Also you are going to get tired of speaking English all the time. I get very tired doing that. I call home a lot and that helps me because I get to talk to people who know my culture and who care about me."

"I didn't understand that I couldn't take a reserve book home from the library and I took one home for the weekend to study. The library called me and made me bring it back— I was lucky—they didn't make me pay because I was a new international student, but you can get a

lot of fines that way. The other students in my class were really angry at me for keeping the book."

"I didn't know where to go to find out about scholarships and grants. Financial Aid and the International Student office are two good places to start. You can also check your own country's scholarships and grants—ask your parents to help if they can!"

"It's really important to hand in your assignments the day they are due. I always take my paper to my instructor to review before I hand it in, to get feedback and help."

"Everyone travels over Thanksgiving, Winter Break, and Spring Break. If you want to go home, or anyplace else, be sure you get your tickets very early!"

"Always make sure you go to class on time! Professors notice if you come in late."

Glossary of Terms and Phrases

Ace: To get a grade of A on an exam

All downhill from here: in the context of a course, easy all the way to the end of the course; in the context of a social relationship, leading toward the end of the relationship

All-nighter, or to pull an all-nighter: stay up all night the night before an exam to study, or to write a paper which is due the next day

Annotated Bibliography: a bibliography which includes references material and also a brief synopsis of the content of the book or article

Awesome: fantastic, very special

Bad: often means its opposite, "good"

Big Brother, Big Sister: upperclassman/woman assigned to you to help you to adjust to campus life

Blue Books: small notebooks used for taking exams

Bomb: to do poorly, be unsuccessful, generally used in reference to exams or dates

Brain: student who is considered highly intelligent

Brew: beer

Buddy, or Bud: a good friend, esp. among guys

Bummer: bad experience or bad luck

Burned out: exhausted

Bucks: dollars

Class Rank: in order of grade point average, your number in your class (for example, 14 out of 100 students)

Come on (to someone): to make sexual or romantic overtures

Come on: a phrase or behavior that is meant to arouse your interest in a particular good or service, often not accurate, true, or reliable

Cool: fantastic, special, very up-to-date

Course Outline: a week-by-week listing of the material required for the course (readings, assignments, examination schedule, etc).

Cram: to study hard just before an exam, when one hasn't studied much before

Curved exam: when all of the exams in a class are graded numerically, the instructor determines the percent of A's, B's, C's etc. in the class and fits the number grades into those letter percents.

Finals: final examinations given at the completion or courses

Flunk: fail

Frat House: fraternity house

Geeks: derogatory term used for people who work and study very hard

Get real: be realistic, not idealistic

Get with the program: be aware of what you are supposed to be doing, what is going on around you

GPA: Grade Point Average

Greeks: members of fraternities or sororities

Guts: courage

Gut course: course with a reputation of being easy

Hassle: something that is annoying or troublesome

Hit the books: study

Hump week: the week that marks the middle of the semester

I.D.: identification card

Independent Study: a planned "course" during which the student works one-on-one with an instructor to learn a particular subject, issue, or material in depth. Student and instructor plan the program of study. Credit is given, and a grade is assigned.

Internship: a paid or unpaid practical experience related to the content of a particular course or a major

Into: intense enthusiasm for something

Intro: introduction, can be used for courses—"Intro to Art" or people

Jerk: a person whose behavior is inappropriate

Lab: a session in a laboratory which is part of the requirement for a particular course, usually a science course

Law Aps: Law school admission aptitude tests

Lower level or Lower division course: a course generally taken by students during their first two years of study in a university

Mall: shopping center

MCATs: Medical College Admission Tests

Mid-term: an examination given about halfway through the term

Nerd: someone who is not good with social interactions

Nickel-dime: to be overly concerned about keeping track of small costs and change

No-brainer: easy exam, course, question

Nuts: crazy, insane, generally not in the medical sense

On the ball: quick and able to respond

Open book exam: an exam during which you are allowed to take your textbook and notes with you and use them to search for answers

Psyched: excited, looking forward to

Quiz: a short test

R.A.: resident adviser, an upperclassman or woman who lives in your dorm and who is there to listen, help, and advise students in that dorm

Red Tape: bureaucratic paperwork and delay

Recommended Reading: reading assignments listed on the course outline which are recommended but not required reading for a particular class

Required Reading: reading assignments listed on the course outline as required for a particular class session

Reserve book: a book which is kept behind the main desk at the library and which may generally be used only in the library's reading room. Sometimes there's time limit on how long each student can use the reference book

Rip Off: cheat or steal

Seminar course: an upper-level course with a small number of students which involves discussion and interaction

Slam: criticize strongly

Slim chance: very little likelihood that something will happen

Super: very good; also superintendent of an apartment building

Survey course: a large lecture course which provides a broad overview of a particular subject area. Usually the first course students take in a discipline

Take Home Exam: an exam which is given to you and which you write outside of class, using any resource desired, usually due back in class at the next class session

Term Paper: a major research report, should always contain footnotes and bibliography

Tuned in: aware of what is going on around him/her

Upper level or Upper division course: a course usually taken by students in their last two years of undergraduate study

Wait List: a list of students who have not been enrolled in a class due to lack of available space, who hope to be able to enroll at a later date

Waive: to be allowed not to take a required class, based on an exam or other proof that content is already learned

Wasted: drunk from too much alcohol consumption

What's Up?: How are you? What's going on?

What's the deal?: What are the arrangements? What is going on?

Wiped out: exhausted

Withdraw: to voluntarily resign from a course or from college
Zoned: withdrawn into self and out of touch with reality around him/her

References and Suggested Readings

American Civil Liberties Union (2001) <u>Know your Rights: What to Do If You're Stopped by The Police, The FBI, The INS, or the Customs Service</u> NY: Author

Behrens, W.F. (1986) <u>Looking Forward, Looking Backward: The Cultural Readaptation of International Students</u> Texas Technical University

Boston University <u>What to Do if a Friend is Raped</u> Boston MA: Author

College Board (2004) <u>College Board International Student Handbook, 17th Ed.</u> Author

Education International (1999) <u>International Guide to Universities and Four Year Colleges in the USA</u> Education International

Educational Testing Service, (2002) <u>Information Bulletin, Test of Spoken English</u> Princeton, NJ: Author

Educational Testing Service (2002) <u>Information Bulletin: Test of English as a Foreign Language</u>, Princeton, NJ: Author

Educational Testing Service (2002) <u>Practice Questions for TOEFL Testing</u> Pricneton NJ: Author

Ezell, C., Clocking Cultures. *Scientific American*, September 2002

Flaitz, J. Ed. (2003) <u>Understanding Your International Students</u> Ann Arbor: University of Michigan Press

Gardner, J.N. & Jewler, A.J. (2003) <u>Your College Experience: Strategies for Success 5th Ed.</u>, textbook and interactive CD-ROM, Pacific Grove, CA: Wadsworth Group

Harbour Group, LLC <u>International Student and Scholar Medical Insurance</u> Reston, VA: Author

Hjorth, L.S. (2003) <u>Claiming Your Victories: A Concise Guide to College Success</u> Boston, MA: Houghton Mifflin

HTH Worldwide Insurance Services <u>Preferred Health Plan for Participants Engaged in International Educational Activities</u> Fairfax, VA: Author

International SOS Assistance, Inc. <u>Scholastic Overseas Services</u> Philadelphia PA: Author

International SOS Assistance, Inc. <u>Welcome to the United States: Medical Evacuation and Repatriation Program</u> Philadelphia PA: Author

International Student Organization, <u>Compass Gold Insurance</u> NY: author

<u>Compass Silver Insurance</u> NY: Author

International Student Organization, <u>ISO Calling Card, with International Rates</u> NY: Author

International Student Organization, <u>VIP + (Visitor Insurance Plan Plus</u> NY: Author

International Student Organization, (Fall, 2002) <u>The International Spirit Magazine: Coming to America, My First Days</u> NY: Author

Kanar, C. (2004) <u>The Confident Student</u> Boston, MA: Houghton Mifflin

Kaplan, (2001) <u>Guide to Studying in the USA: What International Students and their Families Need to Know</u> Author

Koch, N, & Wasson, K. (2002) <u>The Transfer Student's Guide to the College Experience</u> Boston, MA: Houghton Mifflin

Lord, T.W. (2001) <u>The Plan: Medical Insurance for International Students and Scholars</u> Marietta, GA

Luzzo, D., & Spencer, M. (2003) <u>Overcoming the Hurdles to Academic Success: Strategies that Make a Difference</u> Boston MA: Houghton Mifflin

Pauk, W. (2001) <u>How to Study in College, 7th Ed.</u> Boston, MA: Houghton Mifflin

Pejsa, J.(1998) <u>Success in College Using the Internet</u> Boston, MA: Houghton Mifflin

Peterson's (2003) <u>Colleges and Universities in the USA:</u> The Complete Guide for International Students. Princeton, NJ: Peterson's

Prinz, P. <u>Study in the USA: magazines and website</u> Seattle, Washington

San Francisco Chronicle (November 25, 2002) Foreign Student Enrollment Steady Despite Scrutiny, p. A3

San Francisco State University, Office of International Programs (2002) <u>New International Student Welcome Packet</u>

Santrock, J. & Halonen, J. (2002) <u>Your Guide to College Success</u> textbook and interactive CD-ROM Pacific Grove, CA: Wadsworth Group

United States Census Bureau, (2002) <u>Coming to America: A Profile of the Nation's Foreign Born (2000 update)</u> Washington DC: US Census Bureau

United States Department of Justice, I N S (2001) <u>Curricular Practical Training (for F- students)</u>

United States Department of Justice, INS (2001) <u>Optional Practical Training (for F-1 students)</u>

United States Immigration and Visa Regulations explanations, from Boston University International Students Office

> Immigration Rights and Responsibilities of Students in F-1 Status
> Immigration Rights and Responsibilities of Students
> in J-1 "Exchange Visitor" status
> Optional Practical Training
> Curricular Practical Training
> Work Permission for J-2 Students and dependents
> Work Permission for J-1 Students
> Severe Economic Hardship for F-1 Students
> Tax Bulletin
> Alien's Change of Address

United States Immigration and Naturalization Service, Color Photograph Specifications

Some Useful Websites

There are thousands of websites which have helpful information for international students. A select listing is included here to help you get started. Type "International Students in the USA" on your search engine to reach a full listing.

You can also click into your university, city, state, or organization listing for information on events, activities, useful advice, and resources and services.

American Secular Holidays Calendar http://www.smart.net/, holidays and other dates in the US secular calendar

General Information:
     www.StudyAbroadUSA.com
     www.studyusa.com
     www.abroadplanet.com
     www.collegeaps.com
     www.internationalstudents.com
     www.istudents.com

Intercultural Homestay Services
     www.globalimmersions.com
     www.usahomestay.org

International SOS Assistance, Inc. www.internationalsos.com

International Medical Insurance Companies:
> www.hginsurance.com
> www.hthstudents.com
> www.twlord.com

International Student Educators: www.nafsa.org

General Information:
> www.StudyAbroadUSA.com
>
> www.studyusa.com

International Students Chat Room:
> www.iAgora.com
> www.abroadplanet.com

International Student Organization, www.isoa.org

Scholarships and Financial Aid Information:
      www.eduPass.org
      www.internationalstudents.com

SEVIS: legal information about laws and regulations www.sevis.net

Study Skills Sites on the Web:
Your school will have websites which are specific to the requirments of the school.
The websites listed here have been found to be especially helpful to international
students by San Francisco State University's ISSO.

      http://www.keene.edu/aspire/ASPIRE_SS.html
      http://dartmouth.edu/admin/acskills/#study
      http://www.csbju.edu/advising/helplist.html
      http://uark.edu.depts.comminfo/www.study.html
      http://english.upenn.edu/jlynch.grammar.html

United States Government Sites:

http://factfinder.census.gov/ (Census Bureau)
http://travel.state.gov/DV2004.html   (Department of State, Instructions for the 2004 Diversity Immigrant Visa Program)
http:/www.immigration.gov (Immigration and Naturalization Service, for students and exchange visitors)
http://www.ssa.gov/ (Social Security information)
www.egov.immigration.gov/sevis (SEVIS Requirements)
www.immigration.gov/graphics/services/temptbenefits/sevp.htm (Bureau of Citizenship and Immigration Services Student and Exchange Visitor Program Information about SEVIS, emergency travel, naturalization, citizenship, lawful permanent residency, temporary visitors)
www.exchanges.state.gov/education/educationusa (State Department site about educational opportunities in the USA
www.educationusa.state.gov (government Education Department site)

University and College directories and guides:

www.studyusa.com
www.internationalstudents.com
www.americanuniversities.org

Index by Item Number

About the Publisher
The Cambridge Stratford Study Skills Institute

Cambridge Stratford, Ltd. formed The Cambridge Stratford Study Skills Institute in 1985 with the help of its current president, Peter W. Stevens, a former vice president from a private college in New York. It is an international organization of learning and study skills specialists and tutor training professionals dedicated to helping students of all ages to STUDY SMARTER, READ FASTER and SCORE HIGHER ON TESTS, key ingredients for success in school as well as in life.

Cambridge Stratford Study Skills Course System

The CSSS INSTITUTE provides teacher and tutor training services, private courses for students in summer and after school programs nationally, and publishes the internationally renowned study skills curriculum entitled **The Cambridge Stratford Study Skills Course**. It is taught publicly by schools, colleges, federal and state grant programs at 3 levels (6–8th: 20 hour edition, 9–11th: 30 hour edition, and 12–15th: 10 hour edition, entitled *Ten Tips for Academic Success*, available in English and Spanish). These editions include 4 components; Student Workbook, Teacher Manual, Transparency and Listening Tape Set.

Tutor Training Research Study

In 1994, The INSTITUTE introduced a research-based tutor training curriculum nationally under the direction of Dr. Ross MacDonald entitled *The Master Tutor: A Guidebook for More Effective Tutoring*. It includes the state-of-the-art methods tutors can use to improve one-on-one tutoring sessions and consists of a self-instructional Guidebook for tutors, a Tutor Trainer's Manual, and Transparency Set. A pre- and post-assessment, **The TESAT** (Tutor Evaluation and Self-Assessment Tool) is available for validating improved tutoring skills.

Starting 2002-2003, the *Online eMaster Tutor Training Course* was introduced to assist tutor trainers in training peer and staff tutors online. A train-the-trainer course, the *Online eMaster Tutor Trainer's Course*, was also made available to train online instructors in effectively teaching tutors using a hybrid of face-to-face and online instructional components.

Improving the Retention of College Students

The CSSS INSTITUTE's mission is to help students prepare for and succeed in college. In addition to this newest book for international students, three other self-orientation to college books have been published to help traditional, non-traditional adult college-bound students, and online learners adjust to the difficult transitions required in becoming a successful college student. These navigation-to-college guidebooks, *100 Things Every Freshman Ought to Know*, *100 Things Every Adult College Student Ought to Know*, and *100 Things Every Online Student Ought to Know* are suggested reading for all those starting college for the first time as well as those who may be returning to college after a lapse in time. Pre college and college preparation programs may find them helpful in building college persistence and retention among their students since each assists students in understanding college customs, practices, vocabulary, and procedures, plus each includes important tips for balancing responsibilities in college, family, and work environments. New editions of the *100 Things* series are being planned to include disabled students and those in the military.

NOTE: Prospective Authors — The *100 Things* series can be expanded to help others. If you have an idea, book, or concept that might help students succeed in school or college, please contact us at the address on the next page or via e-mail. We're interested!

If you need information about any of the products or services offered or would like a sample lesson (PREVIEW MANUAL) forwarded for your review, write or call today.

The Cambridge Stratford Study Skills Institute
8560 Main Street
Williamsville, New York 14221
(716) 626-9044 or FAX (716) 626-9076
Cambridges@aol.com
http://www.cambridgestratford.com